LOND   BABY
STREETS

BELOVED
LANE

DEDICATION: TO MAMA

LONDON BABY Streets
ISBN: 9781739211578
Published by LANDE Jewels
LANDE Jewels supports professional development of mothers in full time childcare.
www.landejewels.com

THIS READING JOURNEY BELONGS TO

_____

CONTENTS

PROLOGUE

Location of street signs appears child-friendly,
Making it effortless to learn to read the words.
Mother thought the idea was stupendous
And took me to discover street name world.

Filled with the humour, history, surprises,
Adventure lives despite the growing up,
With tens, if not a hundred, thousand entries,
Some unexpected smiles are yet to come.

ODD AND PECULIAR

Pride of the London locals,
Bafflingly labelled streets—

Turnagain Lane, Savage Gardens,
Minories, The Retreat,
Bird in a Bush Road, Cock Lane,
Mount Pleasant, Rotten Row,
Wardrobe Place, Kitcat Terrace,
Poultry, Mudchute and Bow,
Ha-Ha Road, Bleeding Heart Yard,
Crutched Friars, Amen Corner,
Birdcage Walk, Tweezers Alley,
French Ordinary Court,
Man in Moon Passage, Love Lane,
Cockpit Steps, Dairy Close,
Frying Pan Alley, Hind Grove,
Bear Gardens, Sugar Loaf Walk,
Pudding Lane, Fish Street, Rye Dale,
Melon Road, Mincing Lane,
Swallow Street, Hanging Sword Alley,
Upper Butts, Cheapside, Dockhead.

ORIGINS

Before a central body
Assigned unique street names,
The builders and the merchants
Relied on quick-wit say.

They'd give a street a wife's name,
A daughter's or a son's,
Pick tree or fruit, or flower,
Inn, river, public house,
Events that happened there,
The nature of the trade,
Directions, destinations,
Wherefrom and who goes there.

Habitually, the royals,
Nobles and clergymen
Were referenced in naming
Multiple new pathways.

Eventually, the signage
Distinguished street and lane,
The avenue, place, square,
Mews, gardens, yard and gate.

BAKER STREET

Named after William Baker
Who leased and laid the street
To house the upper classes
In comfortable suites.

Baker Street to readers,
Mavens of Conan Doyle,
Who see 221B—fake address,
Consultant detective's home.

Novels inspired the robbers
To pull off a daring heist—
Empty deposit boxes
From nearby Lloyds bank.

Baker Street—oldest station
On London underground,
Welcomes commuters, tourists
Into this part of town.

Waxworks or Holmes' Museum,
Haunted pub, commerce hub
Make worthwhile the ordeal
Of queues, and push and shove.

BOND STREET

Sir Thomas Bond, 1st Baronet,
During Age of Enlightenment,
Built up a fashionable street—
Patrician's establishment.

Traditionally minded shops,
With a Victorian elegance,
Drew in affluent clientele
For hedonist experience.

Prominent names in artists' world—
The dealers, auctions, galleries,
Inhabit both ends—New and Old,
Crowned by Fine Art Society.

The photogenic strip of luxe
Enjoys modern additions
Against the backdrop of the flags,
Sculptures and decorations.

Some come to strictly people watch,
Window shop, phantasise
About the day they carry loads
Of branded merchandise.

CARNABY STREET

Laid out to lodge pest house
During Bubonic Plague,
Carnaby Street resurfaced
As a pop-culture case.

Superstars, New Romantics,
Mods, Skinheads, Punks, New Wave,
Inspired outfit designers
To master fashion dare.

Legendary retailers,
Marked by effulgent past,
Left no trace but nostalgia
For quaint and retro style.

Corridor of stark windows
Resembles outdoor mall,
In contrast to iconic,
Tudor-style Liberty store.

Spirit of Soho mural
Features the local haunts,
Residents, punters, patrons
That public still adores.

DENMARK STREET

Formerly, part of house of lepers,
Goldmine of pestilence and slums—
The only London street that features
Georgian facades on either side.

In 19th century local tradesmen
Concerned themselves with metalworks;
Lovingly nicknamed 'Tin Pan Alley',
Street grew its musical accord.

Instrument sellers, studios, singers,
Settled themselves in Music Land,
Blue plaque remembering 'Giaconda'
Reveals where social talk was done.

Accompanied by Little Tokyo,
Ramshackle single storey homes,
It witnessed criminals in nightclubs
And children living on rooftops.

Vast demolition of its neighbours
Meant local culture hollowed out—
Gargantuan site of brand engagement
Already having an impact.

DOWNING STREET

First private resident on record
Exposed ideas of Guy Fawkes,
King James rewarded loyal favourite
With the extension of his home.

After the heirs let go of leases,
The properties were redesigned,
Foundations—shaken, houses—levelled,
North side begot new cul-de-sac.

Flimsily built by rogue contractor,
A diplomat, kin of knighthood,
The Downing Street, black terraced pathway
Is claimed augustest in worldhood.

First Lord of Treasury, Sir Walpole,
When offered townhouse by the king,
Suggested it be made official
Residence for PM's, not gift.

Barren by double iron gateway,
Tight-lipped and armed policing guards,
Number 10 Downing Street famed black door
Presents obstructed distant sight.

HARLEY STREET

When Second Earl of Oxford
Set to develop land,
He gave his surname, Harley,
To call a street, now—brand.

Synonymous with doctors,
Exclusive private care,
With an array of treatments
To combat a health scare.

Holistic, allopathic,
Nuclear, nano-led,
Are offered in a setting
That patients rarely get.

State of the art construction,
Convenient transport links
Mean the cohort of practitioners
In effect, seldom leave.

HAYMARKET

Continuous maintenance of horses
Around the Palace of Whitehall
Prompted quick-witted pedlars, hawkers
To setup stalls with hay and straw.

The unofficial busy fair
Caused stoppages when pouring rain
Flushed chaff upon the noble dwellings
And cluttered orderly terrain.

Despite the pleas for its removal,
Market remained and Act was passed,
Requiring payment of a duty
Towards the pavement of the path.

In 1830 market perished
To the inhabitants' relief,
The street in the Victorian era
Became gold mine for libertines.

Two theatres with royal patents—
Custodians of performing arts,
Are now supplanted by the restaurants,
Big screens, hotels and novel marts.

JERMYN STREET

Identified with British menswear
And complimentary concerns,
Glorious dandyish affair
Exudes the richness of colognes.

It reeks tradition and refinement,
Groomed visitors add to the art
That boutiques must display in windows
Alongside features of their craft.

Historic perfumer, cheesemonger,
Barber, cigar lounge, private club,
Galleries—drawing dearer, fonder
Afficionados of surrounds.

Modern day urban village
With a Parisian feel
Takes its name from St Mary's
By the stream of Tyburn.

Old church was since demolished,
River and streams subdued
Under a giant sewer
Sir Bazalgette had built.

Centuries of progression
From parlous muddy fields
With savvy execution
Forged prime location yields.

Mix of Art-Deco, Modern,
Georgian, Victorian fronts,
Charms the discerning shoppers,
Real estate connoisseurs.

Summer and winter fairs,
Festivals, Christmas lights,
Market stalls every Sunday
Set neighbourhood to thrive.

MOUNT STREET

A quiet street away from traffic
Was a wise shortcut to Tyburn,
It since enjoyed rejuvenation
With fine boutiques and social clubs.

Facades feature exquisite sculptures
Of Queen Victoria, Prince Consort,
Tables, set for al-fresco dining,
Present a gastronomic fort.

Famous hotel attracts grand tourers
Into a postcard perfect set,
Adorned by silent water sculpture,
That vaporises salient breath.

Shielded by depth of its surroundings,
The garden, former burial ground,
Displays exotics from the islands,
Most notably, a large date palm.

Church of Immaculate Conception
Adds to acoustics with the bell,
While its next door Anglican neighbour
Shines through with golden weathervane.

OXFORD STREET

Famed Roman road to Oxford,
Previously, Tyburn Road,
Witnessed outcry and sorrows
Of prisoners' cohort.

Marble Arch replaced gallows,
Commerce and retail stores
Took over mile-long streetscape
And made it through Great War.

Selfridges and John Lewis,
Jewels of thoroughfare,
Peered at financial ruin
Of neighbouring brand names.

Offering homewares, fashion,
Cheap tat and souvenirs,
Rapidly changing outlets,
Provide mass market feast.

Place of endurance testing—
Litter heck, camps of tramps,
Thousands of stout pedestrians
Merge with the traffic jam.

P ALL M ALL

Merry Monarch, Charles II,
Ordered Pall Mall—play station
For paille-maille, like of croquet,
Amid the Restoration.

The liberated elites
Flocked to new-founded men's clubs,
While capital's fine art scene
Found its base on the expanse.

During the Age of Reason,
Early fertility clinic—
'Temple of Health and Hymen',
Helped the despairing cynics.

Founder of local gas firm
Lit the street-pioneer
For the Regnant's birthday—
Blue plaque spells it clearly.

Oldest arcade in existence,
Brief home to Casanova,
Site of old War Office—
Are secrets the thoroughfare offers.

Park Lane

The Middle Ages saw a rugged track
Along the edges of farmland,
Shielded by brick wall, so onlookers
Won't see the Coppernose's hunt.

Later, the park opened to public,
Barrier was down, railings went up,
Wealthy erected sumptuous mansions,
Houses of substance and the like.

Grandiose suites, hotels, penthouses,
Bedecked for sultans and the sheikhs,
Promote a regular catharsis,
Heed of plutocracy awakes.

Amidst property price inflation,
Sought after address still retains
Campers on grass patch, gangs of beggars,
Rough sleepers in the underpass.

From Marble Arch to Hyde Park Corner
A major transport corridor
Dilutes salubrious Hyde Park air
With growing levels of exhaust.

Picadilly

A rather wide, straight thoroughfare,
Main road to Reading since Dark-Age,
Grew popular when redirection
Took place to mark new Green Park edge.

Prominent tailor, Robert Baker,
Prospered by selling picadills—
Broad cut-work avant-garde lace collars;
The name soon referenced the street.

Home to the celebrated houses,
Embassies, restaurants and hotels,
It boasts flagships of chief booksellers,
Department stores, boutiques, arcades.

It's seldom quiet due to tourism,
Construction work, buses and cars,
Preserving footfall continuity
On stretch length of about a mile.

Gone is St James' Church craft market,
Replaced by take away food tents,
Placed in the forecourt with delightful
Stone fountain and wrought iron gates.

SAVILE ROW

Henry Poole—clothier-legend,
Founded authentic need
For a Mayfair emporium
To suit the men of means.

More ateliers have followed,
Suits, shirts, hats, coats and shoes
Through open basement windows
Come to life in full view—
Colonial, national liveries,
Monarch's robes, costumes, casts,
Military, traditional,
Novel styles—made to last.

Bespoke suite from Savile Row
Is high on a bucket list
Of an aspiring tycoon
Who strives to look elite.

Golden mile of fine tailors
Benefits from safeguards,
Set by a Special Policy
That lauds the timeless craft.

SHAFTESBURY AVENUE

Avenue's arduous path to life
Involved grievous slum clearance,
With the displaced labouring class
Secured in the vicinity.

A certain land had to be set
For their accommodation—
The Board of Works strove to protect
Those in need of protection.

Restriction challenged builders' flair
To contrive proper dwellings,
Later inquest opined land grab
And shady money swelling.

Shaftesbury Avenue was named
After the Earl of Shaftesbury,
Whose dedication to ill-starred
Is, to this day, remembered.

Four theatres on the north side,
Cinemas and chain cafes
Unfold alongside Chinatown
In rapid modernising.

STRAND

From junction at Trafalgar Square
To dragons at the Temple Bar,
Connecting Westminster and City,
Lies 'water's edge', in Saxon—Strand.

Before construction of Embankment,
It was a road right by the Thames.
Blessedly, it escaped destruction
Of all-consuming Great Fire flames.

It carries grand historic buildings—
Somerset House, The Savoy,
Two baroque styled portentous churches,
King's College and The Royal Courts.

It was the first to have house numbers
Starting with 'Number 1, the Strand',
Known for its coffee shops and taverns,
It drew aristocratic crowd.

Two disused stations—Strand and Aldwych
Proved requisite during Great War
For storing rare museums' treasures,
Sheltering subjects from the bombs.

THE MALL

It was a place for croquet-like game playing
For Merry King and gentry, yet it grew
Into a fashionable and inclusive wayfare,
Bordered by trees—a bon ton avenue.

The UK's ceremonial red carpet
Takes pigment from iron oxide,
Offering striking contrast to the park side,
Ivory terraces and Portland stone Buck House.

The route is used for all royal processions
With pageantry and pomp, horses and bands;
The weddings, funerals, parades and coronations
Feature the Mall in prime-live broadcast.

The corridor of flags and decorations
Greets dignitaries and the heads of states—
The visitors and Monarch are escorted
In a state carriage for Palace events.

The Mall stroll offers views of Clarence House,
St James's Palace and Waterloo Steps,
Mall Galleries, Societies, Academies,
And Admiralty Arch crowning its end.

TOTTENHAM COURT ROAD

Referenced as Old Latin Quarter
For classic language scholars spoke,
Named after neat manor of Tottenhall,
Lies spacious Tottenham Court Road.

Dickens, a boy with rare coppers,
A drudge at busy blacking shop,
Frequented locale for some stale buns,
Second-class pastry cooks sold some.

It was a place for piano making,
Woodwork and carpentry until
It landed decorators' mecca
With grand emporia such as Heal's.

Closely, the Middlesex Infirmary
Gave environs regular shocks—
Notorious as a depository,
Collecting corpses for the docs.

Regeneration, thanks to Crossrail,
Cleared up debris of urban spot—
Brutalist Centre Point House
Bejewels plaza, not bus stop.

WHITEHALL

Main residence of English monarchs,
Long perished Palace of Whitehall,
Saw James I grizzly execution
During the English Civil War.

Fire destroyed the lavish structure,
Banqueting House barely survived,
Royals moved out to St James's Palace,
Bear baiting pit—gone from the grounds.

Dotted with ministries and bureaus,
The epicentre of state's might
Is lined with statues and memorials
Including revered Cenotaph.

The citadels of defence centres
Span deep and wide beneath Whitehall,
To public—verbatim off limits,
They serve to keep the nation whole.

Cabinet War Rooms—subterranean
Harbour of tunnel labyrinth,
Headquartered strategy and morale
In darkest days of WW2.

BISHOPSGATE

Originally, an outsider shire,
Area known as Bishopsgate Without,
Developed after devastating fire
And demolition of historic sight—
An ancient gateway into Roman London,
The opening inside the City wall
That closed at night and opened in the morning;
The place is flagged by bishops' mitre stone.

Popular with Elizabethans,
The garden suburb packed with artisans,
Saw wealthy dwellers relocating westwards
And traders setting up ample warehouses.

Victorian and Georgian low rise houses
Remained intact next to back alleys' slums—
Poverty stricken, with excess mortality
They were cleared out and later gentrified.

The Eastern end is intricate in streetscape,
The Western—is important transport hub,
St Bodolph's chyrchyard rests next to skyscrapers,
Train station—onsite earliest Bedlam.

Brick Lane

Countryside field path outside the City
Since Restoration enriched its appearance,
Flemish incomers named street after brick kilns,
Huguenot Protestants brought lace, silks weaves.

Pioneer migrants, diversely Jewish,
Fleeing the pogroms, moved into workrooms;
Growing from rag trade to thriving ventures,
Little Jerusalem turned culture centre.

After Great War, Bangladeshi arrivals
Headed to Brick Lane in search of asylum;
Curry shops sprouted, the fabric shops swelled,
Decor and people produced unique blend.

Banglatown is rife with the layered graffiti,
Suspicious passersby eyeing the witless,
Radical dressers alongside the retro,
Residents who are increasingly gentry.

Authentic pocket amidst growing City
Fights for survival despite barely winning;
Burgeoning cafes and curated markets
Leave truly vibrant fade in the background.

CHEAPSIDE

Cheapside—established thoroughfare,
Had been a market since the Saxon days
Until Great Fire claimed the timber dwellings
Of wealthy craftsmen who sold what they made.

It wasn't cheap in terms of value—
Old English 'ceap' meant merchandise.
It spread into connecting alleys
With its specific enterprise.

Jacobean goldsmith buried treasures
To save them from the Civil War.
Dug out, the hoard amazed collectors
As the best find of Stuart gold.

Birthplace of murdered Thomas Beckett
Is marked onsite by plaque and bust;
Great Conduit signage on the pavement
Seals drinking water channel off Tyburn.

The elements destroyed some churches,
Yet one retains its splendid peal,
Defining birthplace of the cockneys—
Born within earshot of Bow Bells.

FLEET STREET

A former home to national newspapers,
'Ink Street', infamous for its print,
Retains press spirit in historic premises
Despite converting into banks' precinct.

Its name reveals mostly lost river,
Fleet, stretching Hampstead-Blackfriars Bridge.
Largely enclosed in a Victorian sewer,
Its presence can be heard from gutter grid.

First private bank, preceding Bank of England,
Founded by goldsmith and named Child & Co,
From Number 1 served Lincoln's Inn attorneys
And Middle Temple Honourable fold.

Precursor to Madame Tussauds—Mrs Salmon,
Made her waxworks onsite Prince Henry's Room,
The demon barber, Sweeney Todd, quite nearly
Had his tonsorium to shave and groom.

Medieval churches, ruins, serene gardens,
Stone statues, gates, historic pubs,
The shadows of Franciscan friars,
Highlight the thoroughfare's distinctive past.

THREADNEEDLE STREET

The very heart of Roman London
Is rich in diverse artefacts—
Tiles, pavements, coins, glass and frescoes
Were found on Royal Exchange site.

Since Early Middle Ages, Merchant Taylors—
The company, now one of the Great Twelve,
Founded its premises and never changed them
Despite Great Fire and the Blitz illfate.

It is believed that threads and needles,
Associated with the trade,
Gave street its name i.e. Threadneedle;
The trade declined, the name remained.

The rising interest in high finance
Brought great contrivers to the place—
The South Sea schemers, speculators
That saw to public credit strait.

'Safe as the Bank of England' saying
Became widespread when night Picquet—
Household Brigade's select battalion,
Guarded the bank's solid front face.

CHEYNE WALK

A riverside village of palaces
Blooms with wisteria in late spring,
It archives noted olden residents,
Whose art is held in high esteem.

It links the two picturesque bridges—
The Albert and the Battersea.
The moorings on the brownish river
Proffer a floating way to live.

Charming, exclusive, laureled address
Breathes eventful history—
Thomas More lived here in vast house
Until 'Bluff King Hal' dispatched him.

The mews hold remnants of the Tudors—
Mulberries sown by Virgin Queen,
Old garden brickwork, ghosts of stables,
Long whitewashed wall hidden therein.

The Walk includes Rosetti's fountain,
Victorian postbox, the Old Church,
Medieval Crosby Hall restructured
From genuine Bishopsgate home.

KENSINGTON HIGH STREET

St Mary Abbots Church—an ancient parish,
Was occupied since Anglo-Saxon times,
With village along main road out of London,
Dotted with dwellings, hostellers and pubs.

After Dark Ages, plot of land was purchased
By Francis Barry, who began to build
The street about the residential terrace,
Which now is known as Kensington High Street.

It was a fashionable place in 1900's
With indoor market and department stores,
Catering to bohemian subculture,
As well as reverse punks, romantics, goths.

Millenials are seeing fading glory—
Congestion and unmemorable shops
Next to historic architecture icons—
The Barkers, and Derry and Toms rooftop.

East end is gateway to Kensington Palace
And the expanse of evergreen Hyde Park,
The West side features the Design Museum,
Nestled inside the leafy Holland Park.

KING'S ROAD

Merry King's private thoroughfare
From St James' Palace out to Kew
Emerged during a hippie era
With epic counterculture crew.

Chelsea Drugstore, a brushed steel structure,
Offered a local 'flying squad'—
Budding females in purple catsuits
On motorcycles cargoing lots.

James Bond resides off Chelsea's High Street,
The stretch of mainstream and sublime,
With an array of outdoor bistros,
Art galleries, spaces to shine.

Away from overcrowded West End,
It receives much local footfall.
The Garden Centre, fine food market
Welcomes burgess with dogs in tow.

In May, the whole purlieu goes floral
With Bloom and Flower Show delights,
Freshly installed botanic triumphs
Aid sweet olfactory insights.

PORTOBELLO ROAD

A Panamanian outpost
During the War of Jenkin's Ear,
Was won by Admiral Vernon,
Inspired the namesakes a great deal.

Amidst expanse of open fields,
Eponym—Portobello Farm,
Maintained the grazing cows and sheep,
Fed pigs and sold to nearby lands.

As leases sold—houses were built,
In time, the wealthier moved in,
The lane became a market road,
Selling the staples to households.

The merchandise was added to the mix,
The traders offered heirlooms and antiques,
Alongside well worn clothes and bric-a-brac
For swiftly gentrifying working class.

The road meanders past colourful homes—
Victorian terraces upkept with flower box,
On market days it heaves with clientele,
Opportunists and tourists in melee.

SLOANE STREET

Hans Sloane, physician to three monarchs
Is celebrated in place names
Around what once was Chelsea manor—
Cadogan family estate.

It was frequented by Sloane Rangers—
Ladies of English upper class,
Balanced by wellborn Hooray Henrys —
Public school boys epitomised.

The demographics slowly shifted
Towards the Middle East blue blood
Since ruler of an Arab country
Acquired most titles on West side.

London Rodeo Drive is studded
With flagship stores of couture brands,
Historic seven floor emporium,
Embassies, church, hotels and pub.

Rich street, known for its lack of benches
Is undergoing a revamp
That aims to mould timeless appeal
Of green pedestrian boulevard.

CAMDEN HIGH STREET

One of the London poorest suburbs ,
Hood of Charles Dickens' family home,
Saw the prosperity arriving
As the Canal opened to 'town'.

In 1970's abandoned buildings
Were leased to artisans by Board of Waterworks,
A weekend market flourished with the handcrafts
And led to popularity of Camden Lock.

The colourful and vibrant multi-market
Now rife with piercing parlours, ink salons,
Grew infamous so that the Camden station
Had to be closed on Sundays or be blocked.

Road widening and the landscape improvement
Were signs reflecting passing tourists' tastes.
Old buildings were redone, casting continues,
The edge is gone, the trade halls—sanitised.

The vision of the Camden Highline—
Raised park along a disused viaduct,
Shows the pedestrians walking King's Cross-Camden,
Appraising altered High Street from above.

Abbey Road

The site of Kilburn Priory,
A long ago dissolved,
The Abbey Lane—a farm track,
Developed into a road.

Gothic-influenced villas,
Modest post-war high rise,
Witnessed the birth of a legend
In Georgian townhouse.

A global music icon,
World famous for its sound,
Made records of the classics,
Jazz, rock-n-roll and dance.

Renowned for its connection
To peerless Beatles band,
The album cover's crossing
Remains in the limelight.

The daily hoards of tourists,
Devotees and the fans
Mimic musicians walking
In scenic photograph.

Enjoyed the book?

Please, dear reader, stay in touch,
Leave a review or two, share much.
And on that note—goodbye, adieu,
I will be glad to hear from you.

www.landejewels.com/contact

Other Books in LONDON BABY Series

LONDON BABY Christmas
PAPERBACK ISBN: 9798665093406

LONDON BABY Rides
PAPERBACK ISBN: 9798666032565

LONDON BABY Seaside
PAPERBACK ISBN: 9798665082868

LONDON BABY Sights
PAPERBACK ISBN: 9781739211547

LONDON BABY Bells
PAPERBACK ISBN: 9781739211516

LONDON BABY Markets
PAPERBACK ISBN: 9781739211523

LONDON BABY Birthday
PAPERBACK ISBN: 9781739211530

LONDON BABY Wildlife
PAPERBACK ISBN: 9781739211554

LONDON BABY Money
PAPERBACK ISBN: 9781739211561

BV - #0125 - 040324 - C37 - 203/127/5 - PB - 9781739211578 - Gloss Lamination